P9-BIB-143

DISCARD

TRACY SCHOOL DIST

OCT -- 1996

PO24162

BOHN SCHOOL, TRACY

THE SCREWDRIVER

LEARNING ABOUT TOOLS

David and Patricia Armentrout

The Rourke Book Co., Inc.
Vero Beach, Florida 32964

© 1995 The Rourke Book Co., Inc.

All rights reserved. No part of this book may
be reproduced or utilized in any form or by
any means, electronic or mechanical
including photocopying, recording or by any
information storage and retrieval system
without permission in writing from the
publisher.

PHOTO CREDITS
©East Coast Studios: cover, pages 4, 7, 15, 18, 21; © Sears,
Roebuck & Co.: title, page 8; Stanley Tools: page 12; © Tool
Traditions: page 17; © NASA: page 13; © Armentrout: page 10

ACKNOWLEDGEMENTS
The authors thank Airborne Express for their help in the preparation
of this book

Library of Congress Cataloging-in-Publication Data

Armentrout, Patricia, 1960-
  The screwdriver / by Patricia Armentrout and David Armentrout.
    p. cm. — (Learning about tools)
  Includes index.
  ISBN 1-55916-119-1
  1. Screwdrivers—Juvenile literature.   [1. Screwdrivers.
2. Tools.] I. Armentrout, David, 1962- II. Title   III. Series.
TJ1201.S34A76 1995
621.9' 72—dc20   94–46471
                                                        CIP
                                                        AC

Printed in the USA

TABLE OF CONTENTS

THE SCREWDRIVER

A screwdriver is just what it says, a screw-driver. It is used to drive or set screws.

Screwdrivers have a metal blade with a wooden or plastic handle at one end. Some handles are long for a sure grip, while others are short for use in tight places.

Screwdrivers are made with a variety of tips. The size and shape of the tip should match the head, or top, of the screw.

A repair man uses a screwdriver high above the ground to change a street lamp

USING A SCREWDRIVER

All screwdrivers work in the same basic way.

While holding the tool firmly in either hand, the tip of the screwdriver is placed on the screw. The screwdriver is turned to the right to tighten the screw, or to the left to loosen or remove it.

It is important to use the right type and size screwdriver for the job. Using the wrong tool may cause damage to the screwdriver and the screw.

Auto body repair work is made simpler by the use of screwdrivers and other types of tools

COMMON SCREWDRIVERS

The most familiar kind of screwdriver has a flat tip. It is used to turn screws that have one slot. The tip and blade are made in different lengths and widths to fit many sizes of screws.

Another common screwdriver is the Phillips screwdriver. It has a cross-shaped tip made to fit screws with a cross-shaped slot. This type of screw is called a Phillips head screw. The Phillips screwdriver is also made in many sizes.

The two most common screwdrivers,
the flat-tip and the Phillips head

SCREWS

A screw is used to hold two pieces of wood or metal together.

Different screws are made for different projects. There are screws made for wood and screws made for metal.

The top or head of the screw is available in a variety of shapes. There are flatheads, roundheads, and ovalheads. Flatheads are used when joining two pieces of wood. Round and ovalhead screws are often used to attach a metal **hinge** (hinj) to doors or furniture.

The screws on this rain gutter are tightened with a flat-tip screwdriver

A screwdriver is a useful tool when making repairs around the house

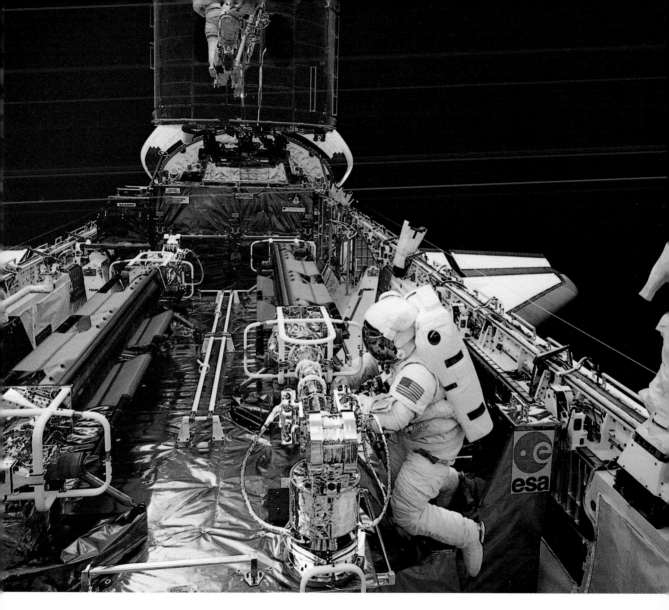

Even a basic tool such as the screwdriver is necessary when working in the space shuttle's payload bay

POWER SCREWDRIVERS

With a push of a switch, a power screwdriver will set a screw in half the time it takes with a regular screwdriver.

Power screwdrivers use electricity to run a small motor. The motor inside the screwdriver provides the power to operate the tool. Cordless models get their power from a battery inside the tool.

Because power screwdrivers save time and are so easy to use, they are used for both professional and home projects.

Tightening a screw on a door hinge is a simple household task

RATCHET SCREWDRIVERS

Some screwdrivers are designed for speed. **Ratchet** (RACH-et) screwdrivers allow a screw to be driven without having to remove and reposition the tool after each turn. This makes the job of setting the screw much faster.

The handle of the ratchet screwdriver locks in place when turning the screw. It then **pivots** (PIV-etz), or turns, to its starting point. The handle can be turned again and again until the screw is set.

It is faster and easier to set or remove screws when you use a ratchet screwdriver

SPECIAL SCREWDRIVERS

There are screwdrivers made for special uses. They are not as common as the flat-tip or the Phillips screwdriver, but they are very useful.

A **jeweler's** (JU-el-erz) screwdriver is small and has a very thin tip and blade. Jewelers use it to work with small metal parts. It can be used to repair eye glasses and other small items, like watches.

There are even **magnetic** (mag-NET-ik) screwdrivers that pick up and hold onto small screws.

An optician uses a jeweler's screwdriver to repair eye glasses

CARING FOR SCREWDRIVERS

A well-made screwdriver should last for many years.

Screwdrivers require little care to keep them in good condition. A screwdriver should be kept in a dry place, such as a tool box or work bench.

If a screwdriver's tip is damaged or begins to show wear, it can be sharpened with a **file** (file). A file is a tool with steel ridges that is used to shape or sharpen hard materials.

Aircraft mechanics use large tool boxes to store and protect their tools

SCREWDRIVER SAFETY

A screwdriver should be handled with care. It is a sharp pointed tool that could cause injury if not used safely.

All tools should be used only for the purpose for which they were designed. Using a screwdriver to pry or pound may cause damage to the tool and, more importantly, could injure the user.

Always wear safety glasses to protect the eyes when using any tool.

Glossary

file (file) — a steel tool used to sharpen, cut, or shape hard
materials

hinge (hinj) — a metal piece used to attach a moving part to a
non-moving part, such as a door to a door frame

jewelers (JU-el-erz) — people who make or sell jewelry

magnetic (mag-NET-ik) — having the property of attracting iron
or steel

pivots (PIV-etz) — to turn on a fixed pin

ratchet (RACH-et) — a device that consists of a notched wheel
that moves freely or locks in place, depending on the direction it
is turned

INDEX